Fact Finders®

The ALAMO

MYTHS, Legends, and FACTS

by Jessica Gunderson

Consultant:
Richard Bell
Associate Professor, Department of History
University of Maryland
College Park, Maryland

CAPSTONE PRESS
a capstone imprint

Fact Finders Books are published by Capstone Press,
1710 Roe Crest Drive, North Mankato, Minnesota 56003
www.capstonepub.com

Library of Congress Cataloging-in-Publication Data
Gunderson, Jessica.
  The Alamo : myths, legends, and facts / by Jessica Gunderson.
    pages cm. — (Fact finders. Monumental history)
  Includes bibliographical references and index.
  Summary: "Explores the myths, facts, and legends associated with the Alamo"— Provided by publisher.
  ISBN 978-1-4914-0204-7 (library binding)
  ISBN 978-1-4914-0209-2 (paperback)
  ISBN 978-1-4914-0213-9 (eBook pdf)
  1. Alamo (San Antonio, Tex.)—Siege, 1836—Juvenile literature. I. Title.
  F390.G89 2015
  976.4'03—dc23   2014007005

Editorial Credits
Bobbie Nuytten, lead designer; Charmaine Whitman, production specialist

Developed and Produced by Focus Strategic Communications, Inc.
Adrianna Edwards: project manager; Ron Edwards: editor; Rob Scanlan: designer and compositor; Karen Hunter:
media researcher; Francine Geraci: copyeditor and proofreader; Wendy Scavuzzo: fact checker

Photo Credits
Alamy: David R. Frazier Photolibrary, Inc., 6; Corbis: Bettmann, 8; Courtesy of The Alamo, 7; Daughters of the
Republic of Texas Library, 17; Deborah Crowle Illustrations, 9; Getty Images: MPI, 26; iStockphotos: xjben, 5; Library
of Congress, cover (middle), back cover, 1 (middle), 11, 18; Newscom: ZUMA Press/San Antonio Express-News/John
Davenport, 16; Photo Courtesy of www.altontobey.com © 2005, 4; Shutterstock: Ann Cantelow, cover (top right), 1
(top right), Arina P. Habich, cover (bottom), 1 (bottom), 3, 29; Texas State Library and Archives Commission, 21, 22,
24; The Granger Collection, NYC, 12; The State Preservation Board, Austin, Texas, 10, 14, 19; The University of Texas
at Austin: Dolph Briscoe Center for American History, 13, 27; Wikimedia: Karanacs, 25; Wikipedia: Dallas Museum of
Art, The Karl and Esther Hoblitzelle Collection, Gift of the Hoblitzelle Foundation, 15, Zygmunt Put, 28

Design Elements by Shutterstock

Printed in the United States of America in Stevens Point, Wisconsin.
032014   008092WZF14

Table of Contents

Chapter ONE

COLONIAL TEXAS

The Alamo brings to mind the glitter of **bayonets** and the thunderous boom of cannon. Men defended the Alamo with their lives to win their independence from Mexico. After the battle, the call to "remember the Alamo!" became, for some, a cry of sacrifice and freedom.

Alamo battle scene

bayonet: a long metal blade attached to the end of a musket or rifle

But this battle site is shrouded in legend and mystery. Its walls hold many secrets. What is the real story of the Alamo? Who were the men who volunteered to defend the **mission**, and what were they really like? Were there any survivors of the battle? Was Davy Crockett really the "king of the wild frontier"? Answers to these questions can be found within the aging walls of this legendary monument.

mission: a church or other place where missionaries live and work

The Alamo was originally a Spanish mission.

The Alamo Then and Now

The Alamo as it stands today surprises many visitors. Most people picture a big, lonely outpost in the Texas plains. In reality the Alamo is nestled along a busy street in downtown San Antonio. Under the bright Texas sun, it can be hard to imagine the brutal battle that took place there nearly 200 years ago. But what we see today is only a remnant of the 1836 Alamo.

Modern-day buildings surround the Alamo's famous walls.

FACT During the Battle of the Alamo, the church didn't have a roof or its famous hump. The roof and hump were added in the 1850s.

The Alamo will forever be remembered as a battle site. However, it was originally built as a Catholic mission. From 1724 Spanish missionaries lived there and farmed the surrounding fields. In 1803 soldiers from Mexico took over the mission and used it as a fort. They named it after their hometown, Alamo de Parras.

By 1836 the fort had several buildings within its walls. Soldiers' **barracks** and officers' quarters lined the walls. The church stood at the southwest corner. Near there, pens housed horses and cattle. The only portions of the 1836 fort that remain are San Fernando church and the lower level of barracks.

barracks: housing for soldiers

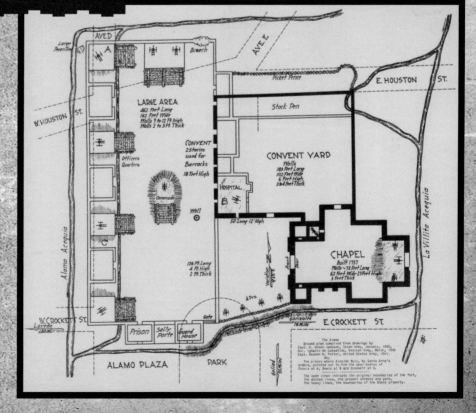

the Alamo in 1836

A Mexican State

In the 1800s Texas was a vast, remote region of northern Mexico. At that time Mexico was under Spanish rule. The Spanish government invited Americans to settle in Texas. The government granted land to Mexican settlers called *empresarios*. These settlers then sold land to American immigrants. The American immigrants were called Texians. They ranched and farmed the land side-by-side with native Mexican Texans, or Tejanos.

Often overlooked is the issue of slavery. Many immigrants were from the American South, and they brought their slaves with them to Texas. Mexico's antislavery laws angered many Texas slaveholders.

San Antonio military plaza, early 1800s

But change was coming. In 1821 Mexico won independence from Spain. The region that is Texas today merged with the more powerful region of Coahuila. This state was named *Coahuila y Tejas* (Coahuila and Texas). Many Texians and Tejanos were unhappy with the new government. They felt that Texas interests were ignored in favor of Coahuila. The government stopped new immigration from the United States. It also increased taxes on the Texians. Some wished to break away from Coahuila and create a separate state of Texas. Others wanted Texas to be an independent country.

The Mexican State of Coahuila and Texas

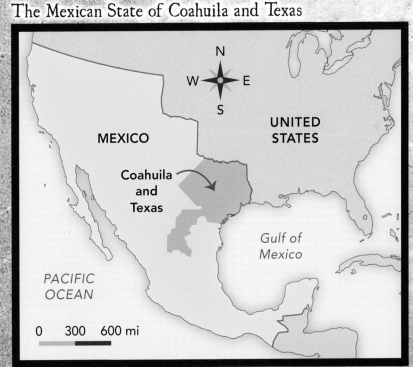

In the early 1800s, Texas was part of the Mexican state known as Coahuila and Texas.

Battle Lines Are Drawn

In the months before the Battle of the Alamo, there were some clashes between the Mexican army and Texian settlers. In December 1835 the Texas **militia** fought Mexican troops at the Alamo. After days of fighting, the Mexican soldiers surrendered. The Alamo was now in the hands of the Texians. No one knew of the bloody battle yet to come.

What happened next changed the course of history. General Sam Houston, leader of the Texas militia, did not think the Alamo could be defended. He sent Jim Bowie, pioneer and soldier, to inspect the site. Bowie and the Alamo's commander, Colonel James Neill, talked. They decided that Houston was wrong, and that they could hold onto the Alamo. If the decision had been different, the bloody Battle of the Alamo might never have occurred.

Jim Bowie

militia: group of volunteer citizens organized to fight, but who are not professional soldiers

Meanwhile the Mexican army was on the march. Commanded by General Santa Anna, several thousand soldiers advanced toward the Alamo mission. They were going to reclaim the mission and stop the Texian rebellion. The columns of soldiers stretched for miles. They had to brave a blizzard that dumped 15 inches (38 centimeters) of snow in their path overnight. Very low on food, the soldiers ate wild plants and small animals to survive. Some of them died. Despite the conditions, Santa Anna urged his soldiers onward.

General Santa Anna

INSIDE THE ALAMO

Throughout January Texian volunteers arrived to help defend the Alamo. They strengthened the mission walls and stocked up on supplies, from food and water to guns and bullets.

But all was not pleasant inside the Alamo. When Neill left, William Travis became commander. Some volunteers wanted Bowie to lead them. One myth is that the volunteers didn't like Travis. In reality they just wanted to be led by a volunteer rather than a professional officer. The two men decided to share command.

The Texians knew the Mexicans were coming to take back San Antonio. But they thought the soldiers would not arrive for several months. Citizens scurried in and out of town, and about 160 revolutionaries rushed to the Alamo. Nearly 20 women and children took refuge inside the fort.

Lieutenant Colonel William Travis with volunteer troops

To the Texians' surprise, on February 23 more than 2,000 Mexican soldiers marched into San Antonio and surrounded the city. But the Mexican army did not attack right away. Instead General Santa Anna raised a red flag over San Fernando church. His message was "surrender or die." Travis responded with a cannon blast, signaling he would not surrender.

Images often show the 1824 Mexican flag (far right) flying over the Alamo. But the defenders may have raised as many as six flags.

Alamo Defenders

Who were the defenders of the Alamo? Many mistakenly believe that they were all white Texians. Largely forgotten are the Tejanos who also joined the fight. At least nine Tejanos died at the Alamo, and many more fought in other battles across Texas.

TEJANOS AT THE ALAMO

Juan Seguin was a Tejano who joined the Texas revolution and went to the Alamo to help defend the fort. Days before the battle, he slipped out of the Alamo to carry a message to the Texas militia at Goliad. When Mexican soldiers saw him, he pretended to be a Tejano rancher. He later led Tejano forces in the Battle of San Jacinto. According to lore, he had the words *"Recuerdo de Alamo"* ("Remember the Alamo") printed on his soldiers' uniforms. After the war, he organized a proper burial of the ashes of Alamo defenders. Unfortunately in later years, his Tejano heritage caused Texians to believe rumors that he was a traitor, and he fled to Mexico.

Juan Seguin

There were nearly 200 defenders of the Alamo, but three men stand out—Travis, Bowie, and Davy Crockett. Myth has built those three into legendary figures. But each of these men came to Texas and the Alamo for different reasons.

Travis was a young lawyer who is often hailed as a heroic commander of the Alamo. He was one of the first to join the Texian rebellion. But he was a slave owner, and he opposed the Mexican antislavery laws.

The Alamo's other commander, Bowie, was a hardy frontiersman from Kentucky. His prowess with a knife made him famous. Some people credit him for designing the wide-blade Bowie knife. However, experts cannot agree on who actually designed the knife. In Louisiana Bowie was involved in **land speculation** and got into trouble for faking land documents. To escape his troubles, he moved to Texas. There he gained further fame for fighting off an Indian raid.

Crockett is the most famous and mythical Alamo figure. He was a pioneer from Tennessee who was known for spinning tall tales. He bragged he could kill a bear just by grinning at it, and he always carried a rifle he called Betsy. Although he had little education, he became a judge and was elected to the United States Congress. After losing re-election in 1835, he went to Texas to join the revolution.

land speculation: buying of land not to use but to sell for a higher price later

Davy Crockett

Siege

For 13 days, the Mexican army laid **siege** to the Alamo. They blasted its walls with cannon. At night, the defenders worked to patch the walls. The revolutionaries got little sleep, and some got sick from lack of food and from **contaminated** water. Bowie became seriously ill and bedridden. Full command of the fort fell to Travis.

Despite the siege Santa Anna's army did let people in and out of the Alamo. Several Tejano women and children were allowed to leave. Messengers slipped past the Mexican lines with Travis' letters to General Sam Houston pleading for help. Travis' most famous letter ends with the words "Victory or Death." On March 1, 32 volunteers arrived from Gonzales. The defenders now numbered about 200, still no match for 2,000 Mexican soldiers.

siege: an attack designed to surround a place and cut it off from supplies or help

contaminated: dirty or unfit for use

William Travis signed this receipt for cattle used to feed troops and civilians during the Battle of the Alamo.

One of the biggest questions surrounding the Alamo is why no one came to the defenders' aid. Some of the blame goes to General Houston, who thought Travis was exaggerating the number of Mexican soldiers. Colonel James Fannin and 400 troops were only 100 miles (160 kilometers) away in Goliad. But Fannin did not want to leave his post unguarded, so he didn't answer Travis' call. In Gonzales, nearly 350 men were preparing to march to the Alamo when they received news of the defeat.

ANGELINA DICKINSON

The youngest occupant of the Alamo was 15-month-old Angelina Dickinson. Travis often played with the baby during quiet moments of the siege. According to legend, Travis carried a gold ring given to him by his girlfriend. As the Mexican troops closed in, he tied the ring to a string and placed it around Angelina's neck. Angelina later gave the ring to her own sweetheart. The ring changed hands several times throughout the years. Today, that ring is on display at the Alamo.

Angelina Dickinson

FACT During the siege, the Mexican army often played music to pass the time. Inside the Alamo, Crockett played his fiddle, and John MacGregor played bagpipes. The two often held musical "duels" to entertain the defenders.

Chapter THREE

THE LEGENDARY BATTLE AND MYTHICAL HEROES

Just before dawn on March 6, a bugle blared. Santa Anna's troops surged toward the Alamo, yelling *"Viva Santa Anna!"* The thunderous sounds startled the Alamo defenders awake. In the darkness they dashed to their positions. Women and children ran for shelter inside the church.

The defenders tried desperately to ward off the attackers. They climbed the walls and began blasting away into the darkness with rifles and cannon. But there were not enough men to cover every inch of wall. Soon the Mexican soldiers scaled the walls and poured into the compound.

The defenders tried to stop the Mexican soldiers from entering the Alamo.

The scene was chaotic and bloody. Gunfire pierced the air. In the darkness and confusion, many Mexican soldiers actually shot one another. The Mexican attackers seized one of the Alamo's own cannon and turned it against the defenders. They blasted apart the doors of the church and barracks. Many lives were lost.

Despite all their efforts, the defenders were soon overrun. After little more than an hour of battle, all the defenders lay dead. The Alamo had fallen to the Mexican army.

All the defenders were killed at the Battle of the Alamo.

FACT Some historians believe 60 defenders tried to escape the Alamo but were gunned down outside its walls. But there is no evidence to support this story.

Santa Anna Cleans Up

As the sun rose over the horizon, Santa Anna stepped into the Alamo to survey the victory. He ordered all bodies burned rather than buried, hoping to send a message to the rest of Texas.

Santa Anna granted the women and children mercy. He let them go free. He sent Susanna Dickinson, the only white Texian survivor, to Gonzales with a message for General Houston. Santa Anna said the same fate awaited the other Texas rebels unless they abandoned the revolution. But Santa Anna's warning had the opposite effect. His brutality in capturing the Alamo united the revolutionaries. Many Americans rushed to aid the revolution.

FACT The number of dead is often debated. At least 189 Texians and 9 Tejanos died defending the Alamo. Between 300 and 500 Mexican soldiers may have been killed or wounded in the battle. Records were not well kept. The Mexican army lacked medical services, and many soldiers died of their wounds.

republic: a form of government in which the people have the power to elect representatives who manage the government

In April Santa Anna marched toward General Houston's army, set up camp, and prepared to strike. On April 21, though, Houston launched a surprise attack. Texians charged into the Mexican camp, crying "Remember the Alamo!" Within minutes, the Texians defeated the Mexican army and captured Santa Anna. The war was over, but the Alamo would long be remembered.

Texas became an independent **republic** and had its own government for nine years. In 1846 Texas became the 28th state in the United States of America.

the official ceremony that made Texas the 28th state in the United States

Chapter FOUR

MYSTERIES OF THE ALAMO

The Battle of the Alamo excited the imagination of Americans and Texans alike. Songs, plays, and novels about the standoff sprang up in the years following the war. Fiction mingled with fact and made the truth difficult to determine.

Eyewitnesses

Eyewitness accounts of the battle differed greatly. The women and children survivors told and retold their stories. With each retelling, the details changed and the story became bigger than life.

Susanna Dickinson told a chilling tale of her experience in the Alamo. During the battle, her husband found her in the church and gave her one last kiss before returning to the fight. He was killed soon after that.

Enrique Esparza

Juana Alsbury recounted that Mexican soldiers stormed into her room, smashed open her trunk of belongings, and stole her money and jewelry. Enrique Esparza, who was 8 years old during the battle, told about an American boy who stood up when Mexican soldiers entered the church. Because the boy was tall and draped in a blanket, the soldiers thought he was an adult and killed him.

Colorful stories such as these became part of the Alamo legend. But were any of them true? Some historians doubt the details because the stories weren't written by the survivors themselves. Instead they were told to others, who wrote them down, but may have added their own spin to the stories.

New York Herald

187 DEFENDERS OVERWHELMED BY 7,000 MEXICAN TROOPS

1,000 Mexicans dead and 2,000 or 3,000 wounded

Headlines from the *New York Herald* and other sources gave very different information about the Alamo.

Santa Anna

70 Mexican Soldiers Dead

300 Mexicans wounded, 606 Texan defenders dead

Deaths of William Travis and Jim Bowie

Mystery surrounds the deaths of Alamo defenders, especially Travis, Bowie, and Crockett. How did they die? The question sparks much debate.

Travis died in the early moments of the battle, but exactly how is a mystery. His slave Joe reported that Travis climbed the north wall and fired at the invaders until he was shot down. But another tale emerged. Some said he killed himself rather than be murdered by the enemy.

William Travis

Bowie was ill during the battle, and most historians agree he died in his bed. But numerous stories about his final moments grew. According to one story, he sat up in bed and shot two soldiers as they charged into his room. Bowie managed to stab others with his knife before more rushed in, killing him. In another story, he was captured, questioned, and tortured by Mexican soldiers before they killed him. Yet another tale says Bowie may have killed himself rather than die at enemy hands. Many historians believe none of these stories. Instead they think Bowie was unconscious from his illness when he was killed.

death of
Jim Bowie

25

Death of Davy Crockett

The most debated and mystifying death is Crockett's. Crockett was famous in life and became even more famous after the Alamo. In the 1950s a fictional TV series about him increased his popularity. Coonskin caps and Crockett figurines became all the rage among youth. Crockett became a brave and courageous American folk hero.

According to popular belief, Crockett fought to the death. In one story, he shot many Mexican soldiers until he finally ran out of ammunition. Then, he used his rifle Betsy as a club until soldiers killed him.

death of Davy Crockett

But in the 1970s, a manuscript by a Mexican officer named José de la Peña was discovered. De la Peña had fought at the Alamo, and the document told about seven defenders who surrendered. According to de la Peña, one of these men was Davy Crockett. Santa Anna did not want any survivors, so he had the men killed.

In 1975 de la Peña's document was published in English translation.

The account has sparked outrage among Crockett admirers. Many refuse to believe that their hero would surrender. Some think the document was a fake. Handwriting experts have found no evidence that the document was faked, although this still doesn't prove the account is true. The debate still rages, and Crockett's death is a mystery that may never be solved.

No matter how they died, the defenders of the Alamo will long be considered legendary heroes of Texas history. However, many people of Hispanic heritage view the Alamo defenders as invaders who did not respect their language and culture. African-Americans do not view the pro-slavery Texians as heroes.

THE ALAMO TODAY

Today the Alamo stands as a reminder of the sacrifice made for Texas independence. But what happened to the Alamo after the battle? Despite Americans' fascination, the Alamo was neglected in the years following the war. Its walls and buildings lay in rubble.

In 1848 the U.S. Army used the fort for storage. Government workers rebuilt the church **facade** and added the famous hump. Then in the 1870s, the barracks became a grocery store. The city of San Antonio grew around the Alamo, all but swallowing it up.

facade: the front of a building

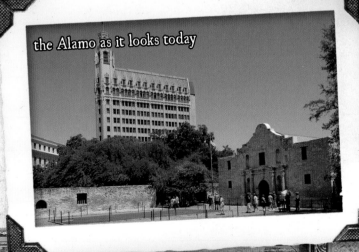

the Alamo as it looks today